Original title:
Melon Melodies

Author: Gideon Barrett
ISBN HARDBACK: 978-1-80586-281-9
ISBN PAPERBACK: 978-1-80586-753-1

Echoes of Lush Fields

In the fields where laughter grows,
Silly critters strike a pose.
Frogs wear hats, the cows all dance,
While breezes play a merry tune by chance.

Bees buzz around like little drummers,
Twirling flowers, sweet as summers.
A piglet spins in muddy shoes,
As flowers blush in vibrant hues.

Harmony of the Harvest

Under the sun, the fruits align,
Oranges giggle, lemons whine.
Apples joke with pears on trees,
While the corn pops jokes with ease.

Baskets rolling down the lane,
With veggies laughing all the same.
A squash slips past in playful glee,
As pumpkins grin, oh what a spree!

A Slice of Joy

A juicy slice brings smiles so wide,
With every bite, happiness can't hide.
Giggling seeds leap from their place,
As flavors dance with vibrant grace.

Fruit forks twirl like little stars,
Creating laughter, with no scars.
Each bite's a giggle, every crunch a cheer,
As friends all gather, the joy is clear!

Nectar's Embrace

Sweet nectar pools in every cup,
Sipping slowly, we all cheer up.
With honey bees buzzing around the scene,
The laughter flows, if you know what I mean.

A splash of joy in every sip,
Witty drinks take us on a trip.
Lime wedges dance and ice cubes play,
As sunshine beams throughout the day.

Cultivating Sweet Dreams

In fields of green where laughter grows,
The fruit of joy, a warm repose.
With smiles like seeds, we plant our glee,
A harvest bright for you and me.

Underneath the shade of giddy trees,
The breeze whispers secrets, carries the tease.
We juggle thoughts like bouncing balls,
Our sweet dreams dance along the walls.

The Taste of Sunlit Days

With yellow rays and silly plays,
We sip the warmth, and giggle away.
A splash of zest on lazy noon,
We're serenaded by a friendly tune.

The sky's a canvas, painted bright,
Each bite a burst, a pure delight.
With sticky fingers, laughter soars,
As flavors tango, who could choose more?

Flavors of the Afternoon

As afternoon strikes its fruity chord,
We venture forth with spoons aboard.
Spoonfuls of laughter, and playful grins,
With every taste, the fun begins.

The table's spread with colors bold,
Each bite a story quietly told.
With every giggle, we share a plate,
In joy, we savor what we create.

Whimsical Watercolors

Splashes of pink and dabs of green,
The canvas brightens, what a scene!
We paint our moods with fruity cheer,
In laughter's hues, we draw quite near.

With brushes made of giggles wide,
We mix the shades that we can't hide.
In every swirl, a joke awaits,
A masterpiece that celebrates!

Fresh Footsteps in the Garden

In the garden, a trip so grand,
Laughter blooms upon the land.
With each step, a squashy joke,
As the dew drops dance and poke.

Bright stripes on fruit, a fetching sight,
Tickled pink, oh what a delight!
Underneath the sun's warm glow,
The giggles and grins start to flow.

The Embrace of Sweetness

A slice of joy on a sunny plate,
With whispers of laughter, isn't it great?
Juicy droplets roll in play,
Cheeky smiles chase clouds away.

Fuzzy skin, a soft embrace,
Sweetness laughs, no need for haste.
With every bite, the giggles pop,
In this party, we can’t stop!

Sweetness Served by Nature

Nature serves a plate of cheer,
Each fruit a story, bright and clear.
Wobbling on like jolly jest,
Funny faces, who can guess?

The crunch and munch, such silly sounds,
In the orchard, joy abounds.
Chasing bees and dancing flies,
All join the feast, what a surprise!

A Tale of Color and Taste

Colors burst, a vibrant show,
Each hue a giggle, watch them go!
A playful taste, a fruity prank,
With every bite, the joy we tank.

In the bowl, a symphony bright,
Oranges, greens, a tasty sight.
From juicy bites, to crumbs so fine,
Each moment shared, is simply divine.

Lyrical Lumps of Fruity Delight

In the patch where the bright fruits grow,
Lumpy shapes with a jolly glow.
They giggle and wiggle, what a sight,
Bouncing around in the warm sunlight.

With seeds like confetti, they twirl with glee,
A fruity festival, come dance with me.
They sing to the sky, oh what a sound,
As they roll and tumble upon the ground.

Serenades of the Early Harvest

Oh, splashy orbs in a sun-drenched field,
Jumpy tunes they lovingly yield.
With every pluck, a silly tune,
Humming along to the harvest's swoon.

They sway in rhythm, a chubby parade,
A frolicsome frolic that will never fade.
They joke with the breeze, a raucous show,
Each one a star in their golden glow.

Dreaming of Garden Feasts

In dreams of gardens lush and grand,
There lies a bounty, wacky and unplanned.
Chubby fruits in a delightful race,
Chasing down laughter, a zesty embrace.

Tables set with the funniest fare,
Each slice a giggle, joy in the air.
With sticky fingers and playful grins,
Every bite is where the fun begins.

A Mellow Chorus in Green

A chorus of hues, all wrinkled and round,
Singing sweet notes as they tumble down.
With smiles so wide, they serenade,
A lighthearted tune in the sunlit glade.

In this orchestra of fruity delight,
Each note is a chuckle, oh what a sight!
They sway with the breeze, in a playful war,
Harmonies echoing forevermore.

Sweet Serenades Under the Sky

In the garden where fruits smile,
Laughter echoes, fun all the while.
Bouncing with joy, they sing at noon,
Tickling the air like a funny tune.

Slices of joy on a picnic spread,
Giggles arise where the fruit's been fed.
Nature's orchestra, a sweet delight,
Sippin' sunshine until the night.

Tantalizing Tunes of the Orchard

From tree to tree, a merry jig,
A soft plop makes the ground do a gig.
The apples chuckle, the berries tease,
Droplets of nectar dance in the breeze.

Underneath branches, shadows sway,
Fruity rhythms join in the play.
Each bite a song, each seed a laugh,
In this orchard, we're all part of the staff.

Dances of the Fleshy, Sweet

Bouncing buddies, what a sight,
Round and juicy, sharing delight.
One slipped and rolled down the hill,
Made the whole crowd gasp with thrill.

With rinds as hats and seeds as eyes,
They jiggle and dance like a sweet surprise.
The ground is a stage, the sun's our light,
In this wacky show, everything feels right.

The Crescendo of Juicy Whispers

Under the sun, the giggles rise,
A symphony of fun in the blue skies.
Each pluck a note, every crunch a cheer,
Juicy whispers, so loud and clear.

They roll and toss in a hilarious spree,
As flavors burst, we all decree.
In this garden of joy, laughter prevails,
With every juicy bite, humor never fails.

Whispering Winds of Fruity Bliss

In the garden, fruits do sway,
With a giggle, they play all day.
Laughter echoes through the vines,
As juicy joy dances and shines.

Breezy whispers, every pear joins,
Singing sweetly, oh what fun!
Cherries chuckle under the sun,
While plums do jive, everyone runs.

Watermelon winks, saying ‘Hey!’,
Can’t resist this fruity ballet.
Each slice a smile, colors galore,
In fruity laughter, we all explore.

Songs of the Summer Feast

Beneath the sun, the feast appears,
Wobbly treats bring laughter cheers.
Peaches giggle, ripe and round,
While cantaloupes hula-hoop around.

Bananas swing on picnic mats,
Telling tales of acrobatic chats.
Pineapples lounge, oh what a sight,
While grapes roll by, bouncing with delight.

Each bite a giggle, a zesty tune,
The tables dance, under the moon.
With forks and spoons, we all unite,
In a fruity symphony, oh what a night.

The Flavor of Laughter

Slicing up a tasty prank,
With juicy jokes, we raise a tank.
Melons tease with every bite,
In fruity giggles, pure delight.

The flavors sparkle, zestful beats,
Tarts and sweets make funny feats.
Each giggle bursts like bubbles of pops,
Delivering joy, it never stops.

Quirky fruit hats played with flair,
Bananas dance without a care.
Silly smiles on every face,
In the laughter, we all embrace.

Choreography of Slices

Chopping beats with fruity flair,
Dance of slices fills the air.
Tangoing zucchinis, pirouette pears,
The rhythm flows, who knows where?

Cantaloupes promise a colorful show,
Sprinkling joy, watch them go!
Fresh fruit bodies in ballet style,
Every twirl brings a fruity smile.

As the round fruits take the stage,
The laughter stirs, it's all the rage.
With each slice, a giggle ignites,
In this fruity dance, joy delights.

Fields of Flavor

In a patch of green delight,
Water drops on fruit so bright.
Silly smiles and juicy bites,
A laugh erupts as joy ignites.

Bouncing beans all in a row,
Tumbling toddlers steal the show.
With each squeeze, the juice will fly,
A splashy giggle fills the sky.

A Harvest Song for the Soul

Gather round, the fun begins,
With fuzzy fruits and silly spins.
Sing and dance beneath the sun,
Who knew that farming could be fun?

Laughter echoes through the fields,
As we pluck what nature yields.
A fruit fight? Oh what a blast,
Memories made, forever cast.

The Sweetness of Late Afternoons

Sunlight tickles every hue,
Colors burst as laughter grew.
With every bite, there’s joy galore,
A treat that keeps us wanting more.

Time meanders, we roam free,
Jokes shared under shady trees.
The day's a party, bright and loud,
Where sweetness grows and dreams are proud.

Melodies Beneath the Canopy

Under leaves, a chorus sings,
Of fruity fun and silly things.
Dancing shadows, bright parade,
Joyful echoes never fade.

With each crunch, a chorus swells,
Together weaving fruity spells.
So gather round, let's laugh and cheer,
Under this canopy, fun is near.

Garden Serenade

In the garden where laughter grows,
The cucumbers dance with silly toes.
Tomatoes giggle, red and round,
As carrots bounce upon the ground.

Bees are buzzing with quite a cheer,
They wear tiny hats, oh so dear!
Spinach sings a leafy tune,
Under the watchful eye of the moon.

Sweet Sips of Sunshine

Sip the juice from juicy treats,
Sticky fingers and happy beats.
Watermelons wear their seeds like crowns,
As laughter tumbles and rolls around.

In the sun, the fruits all dance,
Each one waiting for a chance.
To squirt and splash in juicy glee,
While ants join in with their own spree.

Vibrant Echoes of Earth

Echoing laughter beneath the sky,
Peppers leap, and cabbages fly.
The earth giggles, loving the show,
As radishes shimmy, putting on glow.

Carrots stomp in perfect time,
To a rhythm that feels sublime.
Each veggie sings its daughter prances,
In a world of silly romances.

Rhythms of the Garden Cry

When the sun peeks over the patch,
The broccoli starts a boisterous match.
Zucchini rolls with a twist and a shout,
While nature's chorus joins in throughout.

Fruits of humor in every bite,
With giggles that tickle day and night.
So come along and join the spree,
In the garden where we laugh so free.

Harmony at the Diner's Table

At the diner bright and cheery,
Plates stacked high, oh so merry!
Laughter spills over the sides,
As we tease the chef who hides.

Syrup drips like sweet confetti,
Ketchup smiles, all warm and petty.
The spoon's a dancer, swirls around,
While fryers hum a cheerful sound.

Hats made of napkins, we wear proud,
Joking with the lunchtime crowd.
Grilled cheese sings in buttery tones,
As pickles jam with silly groans.

The jukebox plays our silly tune,
While pie slices dance under the moon.
Surrounded by flavors, we amplify
The sweetest jokes as we munch and sigh.

A Sweet Serenade in the Breeze

In the park where laughter swirls,
Dandelion seeds do twirl.
Songs are sung by bees so bright,
Buzzing 'round, a pure delight.

Picnic blankets, colors blend,
Watermelons on the mend.
Slices carved like happy hearts,
Spitting seeds, oh what fine arts!

Children giggle, running free,
Chasing shadows, a bumblebee.
Every drop of juice a song,
In this picnic, we belong.

As ants march with tiny feet,
They steal crumbs, a sneaky treat.
Summer breezes bring a tune,
Melodies of afternoon!

Juicy Rhythms of Today

Slicing through the sun-kissed skins,
Joy's released, where fun begins.
Taste buds tango, flavors leap,
In each bite, the laughter's steep.

Juice runs wild like a quick parade,
Melodies of the snack brigade.
Stickers on slices, like a show,
What a party as we go slow!

Chefs wear aprons, bright and loud,
Jovially turning every crowd.
We raise our forks, a juicy toast,
To all the flavors we love the most.

The spoons and forks begin to dance,
As fruits unite in a wild romance.
On this plate, we find our glee,
In juicy rhythms, we feel so free!

The Echo of Summer Treats

In the heat, the flavors shout,
Ice cream cones, we scoff and spout.
Waffle cones with sprinkles bright,
Scoop of laughter, pure delight.

Popsicles wobble, colors sway,
Chillin' out on a sunny day.
With each lick, the giggles rise,
Sunshine bubbles in our cries.

Strawberry fields, we roam and play,
Juicy bites, oh what a fray!
Racing with the sweetest treats,
Underneath the sunny beats.

The whispering breeze sings so round,
As sugar dances on the ground.
The echoes of our happy cheers,
Resound through all our summer years.

Notes from the Fruitful Grove

In the grove where laughter grows,
Dancing fruit with shoe-filled toes.
Watermelons wearing hats so bright,
Swinging on vines, what a silly sight!

Cantaloupes telling corny jokes,
Pineapples giggling like happy folks.
The oranges hum a fruity tune,
While cherries polish their disco spoon!

Bananas strut with funky moves,
Bouncing berries find their grooves.
Underneath the sun's warm gaze,
They're hosting the silliest of parades!

So come along, take a peek,
In this grove, it's fun we seek.
Where every bite is full of cheer,
And the fruits all laugh as friends draw near!

The Taste of Warmth in the Breeze

In summer's heart, the fruits all sing,
Jovial notes that make us swing.
From orange pops to pear-shaped sighs,
The taste of warmth fills the skies!

Lemons tell tales with zesty flair,
While peaches lounge without a care.
Grapefruits roll down the grassy hill,
Creating laughs that give us thrills!

Juicy bites with silly names,
Like 'Mister Berry' playing games.
With every pluck, a laugh erupts,
Fruity fun, joyfully disrupts!

So grab a slice, join the jest,
Delightful flavors, surely the best.
In this breeze, pure joy's released,
The taste of laughter, never ceased!

Lyrical Harvest

When harvest time brings sweet delight,
The fruits all gather, ready to write.
A silly song on every vine,
As raspberries dance in perfect line!

The squash provides a base for beats,
While cucumbers tap their tiny feets.
Melodies bubble like fizzy drinks,
Until the laughter just overbrims!

Grapes form a choir, loud and proud,
While watermelons cheer, oh-so-loud!
With every slice, a giggle shared,
In this lyrical land, no one is scared!

So roll with us through fields so fine,
Where juicy beats and joy entwine.
This harvest sings a funny tune,
In fields where summer meets the moon!

The Tune of Summer's Abundance

Underneath the blazing glow,
Fruits create a vibrant show.
Berries twist in tangled calls,
While avocados play with soccer balls!

Pineapples sing from swaying trees,
Laughter carried by the breeze.
Tangerines tap with zestful glee,
Creating rhythms silly as can be!

The citrus sways, a jolly crowd,
With every sound, they sing aloud.
Bananas giggle, taking the lead,
In this fruity band, all hearts agreed!

So dance along with summer’s cheer,
Join the fruits, don't show a fear.
In this joyous, vibrant land,
The tune of laughter's always planned!

The Rhythm of Juicy Delights

In a patch where laughter grows,
A fruit parade, in funny rows.
Bouncing round, they start to sing,
Juicy vibes in everything.

With every slice, a giggle flows,
Flavor spectacles, see how it glows.
Water drips in comical cheer,
Fruits dancing, so we adhere.

When summer's heat comes out to play,
Silly seeds all sway and sway.
Juicy jokes in every bite,
Tastebuds laughing in delight.

Here's a jest, it's time to munch,
Fruit salad now is quite the punch.
With every sweetness, joy ignites,
Come join the dance, oh what a sight!

Sun-Kissed Symphony

Under the sun, the laughter grows,
Nature's orchestra, in funny shows.
Sticky hands and seeds a-fly,
Sipping juice as birds pass by.

A tasty tune, a playful shout,
Silly pips all jump about.
With a twirl and a happy grin,
The juice parade is sure to win.

Sweet and tart in harmony,
Ripe delights for you and me.
Each fruit bursting with a cheer,
Makes us giggle, year to year.

Raise your glass, give a cheer,
To sweet fun that's always near.
A symphony of juicy play,
Laughs and bites, our bright buffet!

Bards of the Bounty

Gather 'round, the bards declare,
Fruits with flair, beyond compare.
Singing songs of zest and cheer,
In every laugh, we hold them dear.

With peanut butter or whipped cream,
Fruity laughter, like a dream.
Savoring bites, we spin and sway,
Bouncing beats on a sunny day.

Dance along with each sweet rhyme,
Silly fun knows no such time.
Pineapples joke and berries chime,
In this feast, we feel divine.

Let's raise a toast to tang and cheer,
Bards of bounty, loud and clear.
With every fruit, a story flows,
In this garden, laughter grows!

Songs from the Vineyard

In the vineyard, jokes abound,
Grapes in laughter, twirling round.
Little bunches sing with glee,
In every note, pure jubilee.

With russet tones, the wine starts to flow,
Tickles and giggles in the glow.
Crushing grapes, oh what a sight,
Squeezed out all our happy might.

Each sip a chuckle, every taste, a grin,
Picking fruit, let the fun begin.
Whimsical whispers of fruity delight,
In our cups, merriment takes flight.

Come gather 'round, enjoy the cheer,
Songs from the vineyard, loud and clear.
With laughter ringing through the air,
These joyful moments, rare and fair!

Summer's Sweet Serenade

In the sun, where laughter thrives,
Watermelons do their jive.
Sliced and served, a fruity feast,
They giggle as they release their yeast.

A picnic spread, oh what delight,
Juicy bites in summer's light.
Seeds fly high, a playful chase,
Kids and laughter fill the space.

Lemonade and shade combine,
While little hands reach out to dine.
With sticky fingers, a cheerful scene,
As crumbs and juice reign like a queen.

So raise your slices, toast the day,
In fruity joy, we laugh and play.
For in the crunch, we find our tune,
Savoring moments from dawn to moon.

The Juicy Whisper

In a patch, where colors bloom,
Fruitiness fills the summer's room.
A whisper soft, a succulent tease,
Water droplets dance with the breeze.

Slicing through with playful grace,
Red and green, a perfect embrace.
Seeds like confetti on the ground,
Chuckles rise with every sound.

Bite after bite, a giggling spree,
The joy of summer, wild and free.
With every chew, a melody made,
Worries vanish, like sunshine's fade.

So we gather, slice in hand,
Creating laughter, all so grand.
In every bite, a tale to tell,
In juicy whispers, all ends well.

Harmony of Rind and Song

Underneath the blazing sky,
Fruitful tunes begin to fly.
Rinds so green, they sway in cheer,
With every note, the joy is clear.

Voices rise, a chorus bright,
As we savor every bite.
Juice dribbles down with a grin,
Lively laughter, let the fun begin!

Ballads sung in sticky hands,
Echo deep across the lands.
With seeds that launch, laughter grows,
In harmonies that joy bestows.

A fruit fiesta, what a sight,
Under moon or golden light.
Every slice tells a tale of grace,
In the harmony, we find our place.

Lush Notes of Nectar

In the garden, melodies sprout,
Frolic and fun is what it's about.
In luscious hues, the feast arrives,
Singing sweetly, alive, it thrives.

Juicy harmonies dance in air,
As sticky fingers rise to share.
Tasting summer, a playful spree,
In every bite, a jubilee!

Laughter echoes, a fruity parade,
With each new slice, fresh plans are made.
We sing with joy, hearts in full bloom,
In juicy notes, we spell our tune.

As the sun dips down with flair,
We toast to summer, free from care.
With rinds and seeds, a merry throng,
In this lush world where we belong.

Chords of Chilled Fruit

A fruit in the fridge, oh what a sight,
It bounced like a ball, such pure delight.
With seeds like confetti, it sings and it jives,
A slice of this wonder, and laughter arrives.

In picnic baskets, it plays a sweet tune,
Under the sun, like a picnic balloon.
With giggles and munches, it twirls on the plate,
Who knew such a fruit could be so first-rate?

Each bite, like a joke, that tickles the tongue,
A melody plucked while the summer is young.
With rinds that are chuckling and juices that flow,
This fruity tune is the best on the go!

So here's to the laughter, the fun, and the cheer,
With fruity performances that bring us all near.
Let's sing to the harvest, bright colors in view,
In the chords of the fruit, we find joy anew.

Lullabies of the Vine

In the garden at dusk, where the shadows creep,
Lies a treasure of sweetness, sugar to keep.
A round little wonder, snug in its bed,
With dreams of sweet juice dancing in its head.

The leaves sway softly with whispers of fun,
As crickets compose under the setting sun.
With a twinkle of stars, the fruit starts to hum,
Lullabies flowing, oh how they become!

Each slice tells a story wrapped tight in rind,
Of giggles and grins that you're sure to find.
Dancing around in the gentle night breeze,
A treat from the vine that brings smiles with ease.

So don't close your eyes, let the fruit serenade,
Its juicy crescendos, a playful parade.
With laughter on lips, we embrace every bite,
In lullabies bursting with pure delight.

Crescendo of Refreshment

Beneath the hot sun, a treat takes the stage,
With laughter, it bursts from its juicy cage.
Each slice a crescendo, a splash and a spout,
In the chorus of summer, it sings loud and out.

A splash in the pool, a freeze on the tongue,
With giggles that echo, this fruit's never done.
It twirls with the laughter, it dances around,
A symphony sweet where pure joy is found.

Across crowded tables where friends gather close,
This fruit of enjoyment, it matters the most.
With hiccups of joy and sweet melon cheer,
A refreshing delight that we hold oh so dear.

So raise up your forks and let's chime in the fun,
With slices of laughter, the day's just begun.
This vibrant crescendo, of flavor and glee,
Refreshment in bites, come taste it with me!

The Taste of Sweetness

A bowl full of laughter, a feast for the eyes,
With colors so bright, oh, how time flies.
Beneath all the laughter, a hidden surprise,
Each bite brings a grin, as joy multiplies.

With dribbles and giggles, we share it with friends,
The sweetness of life, where the fun never ends.
A splash on the tongue, like tickles that play,
In this world of delights, who could ever say nay?

Each bite is a whisper, an invitation to cheer,
Bringing everyone close, love and laughter appear.
With the crunch and the squish, it's a dance in our hearts,
An orchestra vibrant, where humor imparts.

So savor the sweetness from ripe summer trees,
With a splash and a grin, let's enjoy in the breeze.
From juice that runs wild, to laughter's embrace,
This taste of sweet moments we joyfully chase.

Tunes from the Summer Patch

In a patch where laughter grows,
Water droplets play with toes.
Bouncing seeds in rhythm dance,
Swaying leaves in nature's prance.

Cucumbers join with silly grins,
Radishes test their wobbly spins.
Zucchinis sing in high-pitched glee,
The corn shimmies like a bee.

Bees buzz loudly, set the stage,
They write songs upon a page.
With each pluck of juicy fruits,
Giggles run in hearty toots.

A slice of sun, a splash of cheer,
Watermelons roll, bringing beer.
In the summer patch they sway,
Funny tunes light up the day.

Divas of the Fruit Bowl

In the bowl, a fruity crew,
Berries blush in vibrant hue.
Kiwi struts with fuzzy flair,
Bananas toss their hair with care.

Grapes share gossip, oh so sweet,
Lemon sings, a tangy beat.
Pineapple spins in golden light,
Peach shows off her juicy bite.

Raspberries laugh, tickle with zest,
Cherry winks, she's simply the best.
Each diva beams in fruity grace,
As they dance in this bowl space.

Lime joins in with a zesty jibe,
Making melodies that will vibe.
In this bowl, the fun won’t cease,
Laughing fruits bring us such peace.

Refreshing Harmonies

Splashing sounds of summer air,
Fruit juices mix without a care.
Watermelon tunes delight,
Rhythms burst at every bite.

Mint leaves whistle, fresh and bright,
Popsicles twirl with sheer delight.
Cantaloupe hops with glee,
Shaking hands with a honey bee.

Smoothies sing in blenders' hum,
Strawberry joins with a big drum.
Chill breeze carries the sound near,
As laughter dances, loud and clear.

Every sip a joyful cheer,
Nature’s bounty that we hold dear.
Refreshing notes delight the crowd,
Making summer feel so proud.

Serene Harvest Tales

In fields where laughter seeds are sown,
Whispers weave in winds alone.
Harvest carts roll down the lane,
With funny tales, we break the plain.

The pumpkins giggle, round and wise,
While carrots share their crisp surprise.
Squashes croon a mellow song,
As the harvest drags along.

Beneath the sun, we slice and scoop,
Zucchinis join in the happy troupe.
Every tale a punchline sweet,
Harvesting joy with every treat.

In twilight's glow, we gather near,
Sharing scoops, and jokes bust here.
Serene tales twinkling full of cheer,
Fruitful laughter, all we hold dear.

Serenade of Summer's Bounty

Juicy spheres sit on the table,
Wobbling next to a care-free fable.
With every bite, a splash of cheer,
Spilling giggles, laughter near.

Seeds like treasures in greenish rooms,
Popping out like tiny balloons.
Each slice a story, a silly jest,
In the heat, we dance and rest.

A feast of colors, vibrant display,
Who knew fruits could dance and sway?
Lemonade laughs in the bright sun,
Making everyday a bit more fun!

The juicy joys under blue skies,
Tickling tongues, oh what a prize!
Summer’s laughter in every bite,
Fruits and friendship, pure delight!

The Orchard's Gentle Anthem

Whispers of sweetness float in the air,
As critters dance without a care.
With every munch, the giggles rise,
Underneath the sunny skies.

Round and plump, they're quite the show,
Rolling ‘round just like a pro.
A comical crunch in every part,
Fruits bursting forth, steal the heart.

Jesters in skin of orange and green,
Chasing shadows, wild and keen.
Laughter echoed in orchard lanes,
Nature plays its funny games.

When colors blend in sweet delight,
Each fruity moment feels just right.
So gather round for the joyful feast,
Where every bite’s a laughter beast!

A Symphony of Ripe Fragrance

Harmony in the sunlit grove,
Bouncing flavors deftly wove.
Scented laughter hangs soft and sweet,
The silly tang of nature's treat.

Fruity antics, oh so clever,
Shining in the sun, forever!
Lemonade spills, giggles bloom,
Nature thrusts us into the room.

Colors splash like a painter's dream,
Creating chaos like whipped cream.
Each bite a note in a funny tune,
Playing joy beneath the moon.

Dancing leaves and shimm'ring light,
Each fruity flavor ignites the night.
In this orchestra of glee,
We hum along, wild and free!

Melodies of the Sun-kissed Fruit

Dancing fruits sway on a branch,
Making passersby take a chance.
What's this magic hanging low?
Time for laughter, let's all go!

The juicy tales that they unfold,
In summer's warmth, let wonders hold.
Every crunch brings forth a rhyme,
Tasty giggles, oh what fun time!

Chasing seeds like playful sprites,
Jumping around in joyful heights.
Each bite sings a merry tune,
Underneath the smiling moon.

Sweets and laughter in every way,
Bringing sunshine to the day.
So gather round, in joyful spree,
Where fruits and laughter sing with glee!

Whispers of the Orchard

In the orchard where laughter grows,
Fruits giggle as the cool breeze blows.
Watermelons wear hats quite askew,
Chasing sunlight just like the dew.

The pumpkins laugh at a joke of squash,
Dancing around in a playful posh.
Bees buzz in tune, like a silly band,
While cherries throw pits just to make a stand.

Apples in baskets play hide and seek,
Pears try to roll, but they're too meek.
Grapes swing on vines like they're on a ride,
And plums take a tumble, with laughter as guide.

Lemonade laughter spills in the sun,
While a cantaloupe claims it's second to none.
In this orchard, joy always finds space,
Where fruits have a party, a merry old place.

Sunset in a Seed

A sunbeam flicked a seed on the ground,
Said, "Come dance with me, we'll spin around!"
The peaches giggled, plump and lush,
While strawberries blushed in a charming hush.

Out in the field, a cucumber yawned,
He claimed to have grown too quickly and honed.
Tomatoes rolled over, bright and red,
Singing, "Get up! There's fun to be spread!"

As shadows grew long, the veggies would cheer,
While pumpkins declared, "We have nothing to fear!"
Each seed held a secret of joy to unfold,
In the sunset's warm touch, stories untold.

They danced through the twilight, a whimsical sight,
Roots tapping to melodies, hearts feeling light.
Under soft starlight, they laughed and they swayed,
A symphony born of the games they had played.

Sweet Juices of Summer

Chillin' in shades, with a slice of delight,
Juicy fruits giggle, so fresh and so bright.
Lemonades splash while the kids run around,
Watermelon whispers, "Best taste to be found!"

Peach pies are bouncing, all fluffy and round,
While zesty limes are making silly sounds.
The prancing berries joined in the mix,
They jive to the tunes, pulling off funny tricks.

Ice cream cones tumbled down sandy shores,
As cherries went splat like tiny wild roars.
A feast full of laughter and laughter galore,
In this summer party, who could wish for more?

As evening creeps in, with fireflies in tow,
Nectarines grin, "We're the stars of the show!"
So raise up your glasses, gather 'round, dear,
For the sweetest of juices is here to bring cheer.

The Serenade of Green Rinds

In the garden, green bands play their tune,
With a caper here and a jig under moon.
Lettuce twirls, in a dress made of leaf,
Pumpkin's so proud, it declares, "I'm the chief!"

Cucumbers join in, bringing rhythm so cool,
Zucchini's a star, making waves in the pool.
Tomatoes throw salsa, leading the dance,
While radishes chuckle, "Let's give it a chance!"

Under the stars, with each note they share,
A broccoli solo that makes you want to stare.
With laughter and veggies, the night drips with glee,
Embracing the flavors so wild and so free.

In this merry garden, no hunger in sight,
Every fruit and veggie sparkles so bright.
So join in the chorus, don't let it unwind,
For the rinds sing a serenade, funny and kind.

Echoes of Ripened Bliss

In the patch where shadows play,
Laughter bounces, bright and gay.
Round and plump, a fruity cheer,
Let's all sing, the time is near.

Seeds that twinkle in the sun,
Jokes and giggles, oh what fun!
Slice it thick, and hear the sound,
Joyful crunching all around.

Bold and sweet, a summer tune,
Dancing with the afternoon.
Gleeful grins and sticky hands,
Life is great in these lush lands.

So let's sip and make a toast,
To the fruit we love the most.
With every bite, we feel the bliss,
In this melody, we can't miss!

The Lullaby of Green and Gold

Underneath the leafy shade,
A silly serenade is played.
Bouncing sounds of laughter rise,
As sunlight dances in the skies.

Chunky bites of joy unite,
We smile wide, what a sight!
Rinds that shine in colors bright,
The sweetest treat, a pure delight.

Giggles echo through the grove,
With every taste, the fun we wove.
Chasing shadows, darting round,
Is this fruit, or magic found?

Sing along, let voices swell,
In this garden, all is well.
A symphony of juicy bliss,
In every crunch, we find our kiss!

Sweetness on the Breeze

A gentle waft, a fragrant air,
Bringing joy without a care.
Little seeds, a dance they twirl,
In this world, how they unfurl!

Tickled toes in grassy fields,
Laughter blooms as nature yields.
With every slice, a burst of cheer,
In every giggle, summer's near.

Whispers soft, a playful rhyme,
As we savor, lost in time.
Carved in shapes, a joyful spree,
Nature's gifts, oh how they please!

Join the fun, don't take a pause,
In our bounty, life's applause.
With every munch, our hearts fall free,
Sweetness carried on the breeze!

Chords of Refreshing Delight

Harmony of taste and cheer,
Melodies that feel so near.
Juicy notes, so crisp and bright,
Dancing through the sunny light.

Plays of colors greet the eyes,
A funny tune that never lies.
Slice it up, with laughs we sing,
Oh, the joy that fruits can bring!

Pitter-patter, water’s song,
In the sun, we all belong.
Chords that echo, sweet and clear,
Bring us joy, let’s all cheer!

So gather ‘round, we won’t be shy,
With every bite, let spirits fly.
In this anthem of delight,
We’ll savor fun from morn till night!

Melodic Days of the Vineyard

In the vineyard, grapes do groove,
Dancing vines make the bubbles move.
Squishy feet on a juicy floor,
Laughter echoes, who could ask for more?

Grape pickers sing with silly flair,
Wobbling hats, a quirky pair.
Joking fruits hanging from the vine,
Tickling souls with bubbles of wine.

Rows of green in a playful line,
Each step taken, a wobbly sign.
Drunk on laughter, slipping away,
Bottles of joy in bright array.

As day turns to night, the fun won't hush,
Grape juice toasts in a flavorful rush.
With every sip, the giggles grow,
For in this vineyard, laughter's the show.

Seasonal Songs of Soft Delights

In springtime blooms, the fruits take stage,
Ticklish breezes, a merry age.
Strawberry hats and cherry shoes,
Silly songs in the morning dew.

Summer brings a juicy spree,
Watermelon smiles, wild and free.
Giggling children at picnic tables,
Slicing fruit, their laughter enables.

Autumn leaves with a fruity twist,
Pumpkin patches join the list.
Squash jokes flying through the air,
Harvest fun beyond compare.

Winter whispers, sweet and bright,
Citrus dreams in the frosty night.
Sipping cider, hearts feel light,
Merry melodies take flight.

Cherry Blossoms and Citrus Sounds

In a garden of laughter, blooms so bright,
Apples giggle, lemons take flight.
Pineapples wear hats, looking quite grand,
As oranges dance in a fruit-filled band.

Cherry blossoms chuckle, a soft breeze flows,
While cantaloupes hide in the flower's rose.
Grapes juggle softly, what a funny sight,
In this fruity fiesta, everything feels right.

Peaches and plums play cards in the shade,
Laughing so hard, their worries allayed.
Bananas slip by, in a yellow parade,
Creating a symphony, no choice but to stay.

So here in the orchard, joy will abound,
With cherry blossoms and sound all around.
Each fruit's silly antics, a delightful find,
In this quirky haven, let laughter unwind.

Notes from the Picnic Table

Underneath the old oak, we spread our spread,
Watermelons giggle, and play peek-ahead.
A strawberry whispers a funny old tale,
While cantaloupes wind up, setting sail.

Lemons throw jokes like fizzy confetti,
Oranges chime in, 'Come on, it's ready!
The ants are all dancing, a clumsy ballet,
While pickles are singing, 'Please join the fray!'

The biscuits are rocking, a real soft shoe,
Pommes dance with style, on the picnic cue.
Cabbages wobble in their own little spree,
As carrots crack jokes, like it's comedy 'C.'

Each bite's a delight, with stories to tell,
Underneath the old oak, all's merry and swell.
In fruits' funny stories, we'll surely delight,
On this picnic table, everything feels right.

Fruitful Melodies Unspooled

In the orchard of laughter, notes fly like birds,
A bunch of ripe berries compose silly words.
The plums strum their bass, while cherries hum high,
As bananas groove beneath the blue sky.

Grapefruits whiffle, their peels play a tune,
Zucchinis whistle sweetly in afternoon.
Figs tap their toes, in a dance with delight,
Creating a vibe that feels just right.

Kiwis bounce around with zesty glee,
Melting into laughter, as juicy as can be.
A pear on a piano, playing soft and sweet,
While apples throw confetti, not missing a beat.

So sing with the fruits, let your worries go,
In this vibrant playground where the silly flow.
Each melody sprouting, in the sun's warm embrace,
Unspooling joy, in a fruity ballet space.

Afternoon Echoes in the Shade

In the dappled shade, a gathering's begun,
Peaches trade puns; it’s all in the fun.
Lemons tell stories that twist and renew,
While coconuts giggle, just piling on you.

Watermelons roll with a boisterous cheer,
As limes share their secrets, whispering near.
The grapes make a racket, a playful parade,
While figs and bananas join in the charade.

Cantaloupes play hopscotch on circular ground,
Laughing aloud as their flesh is unbound.
Papayas are juggling, a spectacular show,
While cherries chant anthems, ‘Let’s go with the flow!’

So gather the fruits, let the echoes resound,
In this humorous choir, joy knows no bound.
With laughter and sweetness, the afternoon sways,
In echoes of fun, in the sunlight's warm rays.

Harmony Among the Vines

In fields where laughter grows,
The vines twist high in rows.
Fruit hangs with a silly grin,
Beneath the sun, let the fun begin.

A critter hops, it makes a dash,
Chasing chunks, oh what a smash!
Giggles echo through the air,
Nature's joke is everywhere.

With every bite, a juicy cheer,
Squeezes out a friendly sneer.
The taste of joy, the crunch of glee,
Oh sweet vine song, come dance with me!

As twilight whispers, shadows play,
We munch on laughter, come what may.
In a world with bursts so bright,
We'll savor joy, all through the night.

A Tapestry of Sweets

Threads of sugar in the air,
Sticky fingers everywhere.
The tapestry of taste unfolds,
With giggles bright and tales retold.

Fruity friends, a riotous crowd,
Bouncing about, oh so loud!
Colors splash, a playful sight,
As smiles bloom in pure delight.

Drizzles of honey, bursts of zest,
In this feast, we are the guests.
Sticky joy on every cheek,
With belly laughs, we feel unique.

As laughter weaves through every bite,
These sweet connections feel just right.
We dance and hop, a silly spree,
In this banquet of giggles, we roam free.

The Taste of Dusk

As day wanes, we gather round,
With fruity feasts, what joy we've found!
The sunset plays, with colors bold,
In twilight's grip, laughter unfolds.

Nibbling softly, what a treat,
Each bite dances, light and sweet.
Stories spill like juicy drops,
Under the sky where laughter hops.

Chasing dusk with every taste,
Sweet surprises we can't waste.
With each giggle, the stars align,
In dusk's embrace, we sip on wine.

So raise a slice, let's toast the night,
In fruity flavors, everything's right.
With laughter echoing, we'll explore,
The taste of dusk, forevermore.

A Symphony of Soft Skin

A gentle touch, oh so divine,
With soft skin fruits that intertwine.
Ticklish bites and funny sounds,
In this adventure, laughter abounds.

Glistening gems on softest beds,
Silly games in our happy heads.
Squishy laughs and playful bites,
Delightful mischief in starry nights.

Squeezed embraces, giggling glee,
In every fruit, a symphony.
With whispers sweet and playful grace,
We'll dance in joy, at our own pace.

So gather round, let's celebrate,
With fruity fun that's truly great.
A symphony of joy, we'll find,
In every bite, our souls aligned.

Rhapsody in Pink

In a patch so bright, they laugh and play,
Round little seeds, they dance all day.
With skins so smooth, a joyful sight,
They jiggle and wiggle, oh what a delight!

Bouncing from vine, they pop with cheer,
Spitting out seeds, let's make it clear.
The juice runs sweet, it's sticky fun,
Summer's the season; oh, let’s run!

Each slice a grin, giggles in the sun,
A splash of pink, so sweetly spun.
Eating with friends, laughter galore,
A fruity party, who could ask for more?

So raise a fork to this fruity score,
With juicy bites, we always want more!
In pink we sing, with each little bite,
A rhapsody bright, oh what pure delight!

Ode to the Golden Flesh

Golden orbs in the midday sun,
Their juicy goodness is hard to shun.
With a wink and a slice, they beckon us near,
Let's feast on this treasure, oh my dear!

Rolling around, they greet with glee,
A burst of sunshine, so wild and free.
We munch and we crunch, the world feels right,
With golden bites that make hearts light.

Laughter erupts with every rich taste,
No time to waste, come join the feast!
Slip and slide in the sticky sweet,
A carnival treat, oh what a feat!

So here's to the flesh that's golden and bright,
With every juicy bite, we share delight.
An ode to the flavor, let's sing with zest,
In every slice, we find our best!

Soft Beats of the Grove

In the heart of the grove, a rhythm plays,
With fruits all around, they sway and amaze.
Each beat it drops, a giggle, a grin,
As juices flow down, let the fun begin!

Bouncing branches bearing sweet tunes,
Join in the dance beneath the moons.
We whistle and hum, in harmony's flow,
With soft beats ringing, we'll never slow!

Sticky and sweet, oh what a sight,
Chomping on pieces, everything feels right.
With friends by our side, and rhythm divine,
The grove's lively song, it's truly our time!

So raise your voice to the fruits so merry,
With laughter and joy, let’s dance and be merry.
Soft beats of the grove, let's celebrate,
In this fruity dream, we find our fate!

Notes of Nature's Treats

Flavors collide in a zesty tune,
Nature's own candy, beneath the moon.
With colors so bright, they dance on the tongue,
In this fruity chorus, forever we're young!

Each little bite, a note so sweet,
A symphony crafted from nature’s beat.
With laughter and joy wrapped up in each slice,
Peeling away worries, oh, isn’t it nice?

On picnic blankets, we gather and share,
Notes of delight float light in the air.
With fruity percussion, we clap and we cheer,
A concert of treats that brings us all near!

So take a big bite, let the music resound,
In nature's sweet orchestra, joy can be found.
Notes of indulgence, we’ll never retreat,
With every new fruit, life feels complete!

Harmonies of Nature's Sweetness

In the garden, fruits do sway,
With every breeze, they dance and play.
Laughter bubbles with each bite,
Sugar drips, pure delight.

Juice spills down in bright delight,
As bees hum tunes from morn till night.
Silly faces, seeds in tow,
Nature's sweetness steals the show.

Colors burst like laughter loud,
Underneath the leafy crowd.
Each fruit a jester, ripe and round,
Frolicking joyously, it’s found!

Chasing each with giggles free,
A carnival of taste, you see.
Harmonies weave through the air,
While we munch without a care.

Echoes of a Orchard's Heart

In orchards wide, the fun begins,
Where every fruit wears silly grins.
Oranges juggle, apples twirl,
Nature's circus starts to whirl.

Crisp and juicy, they all shout,
“Take a bite, don’t be without!”
Fruits in costumes, oh so bright,
Launching seeds in a playful flight.

A wind-up laugh, a berry tease,
Each fruit a joke, an easy breeze.
Hushed whispers of the joyful trees,
Echo dreams that float like bees.

With every munch, a riddle’s spun,
To taste the magic, oh what fun!
The orchard sings in colors bold,
As sweetly silly tales unfold.

A Dance of Citrus and Sweetness

Citrus twirls with a zesty gleam,
Jazzy flavors join the theme.
Bananas slip and slide around,
Their natural rhythm knows no bound.

Ripe and ready for a cheer,
Fruitful jests are always near.
Lemons laugh, their tang a joke,
While honeydew plays in the smoke.

Skip and hop, the berries jig,
A fruity dance, a bold new gig.
Juicy verses spin and roll,
In a funny fruit parade, we stroll.

Dance along, the laughter soars,
In every bite, a cousin roars.
With citrus kisses, vibrant and bright,
Each moment's tasty, pure delight!

Reverie of the Ripened World

In a world where sweetness reigns,
Laughter spills from juicy veins.
Plump and ripe, the fruits declare,
"Join the feast, we're beyond compare!"

Mirthful grapes in shades of jest,
Welcoming all to their fruity fest.
Limes and peaches in a race,
Rolling laughter in every place.

Silly seeds with tales so grand,
Bounce around in nature's band.
Watermelons play peek-a-boo,
Bringing smiles to me and you.

Each slice a story, bright and clear,
In ripened worlds, we share a cheer.
Funny fruits, a giddy swirl,
In reverie, we laugh and twirl.

Rhythms in the Garden

In a patch of green, they sway and jig,
Round and round, a fruity gig.
With laughter loud, they roll and slide,
In the soil, their secrets hide.

The sun beats down, they glisten bright,
Wobbling in their summer flight.
With every step, a squishy sound,
A playful dance on solid ground.

Crows look on, with puzzled caws,
At fruits that laugh without a cause.
Bouncing here and bouncing there,
The garden's filled with fruity flair.

Peeking through the leaves, they tease,
Making sure they catch the breeze.
With every giggle, juice does flow,
Sprinkling joy like rainbows glow.

Frosted Fables of Summer

Under the sun, a tale unfolds,
Of scrappy seeds and tales retold.
With frosty hats, they strut around,
In a world where fun is found.

Whipped up dreams in fruit sorbet,
Chuckle as they play all day.
A pop of color, a dash of flair,
Laughter echoes in the air.

Dancing spoons with dulcet tunes,
Wobbling fronds beneath the moons.
They tap and swirl, with giggles bright,
Making mischief in the night.

Gliding on a dish half-full,
With frosted tales that start to pull.
In sticky sweetness, joy takes flight,
A summer's dream, a pure delight.

The Whistle of Juicy Joy

Beneath the sky, a playful sound,
Juicy whispers swirl around.
With every hiccup, laughter grows,
A tune that only nature knows.

Slipping seeds and giggling bites,
Dancing ‘round in funny tights.
Each bubble burst, a melody,
Singing sweetly, wild and free.

The breeze joins in, a vibrant hum,
As fruity treasures start to drum.
With every plop, a note is struck,
In this symphony of pure luck.

Chiming chimes, they twirl and spin,
A juicy jig, let the fun begin!
With laughter loud, they sip and slurp,
In a world where joy does burp!

Vibrations of Nature's Treat

In a garden bright, where giggles grow,
Fruits vibrate with a bouncy glow.
With a tickle here and a twisty turn,
They bounce and bounce, for joy they yearn.

Crisp and sweet, they leap with glee,
A juicy waltz, come dance with me!
With every bounce, a splash of fun,
In the warmth of the shining sun.

Whirling shapes in hues so bright,
Crafting moments, pure delight.
With every laugh, flavors burst,
In this candy land, we're lovingly cursed.

So join the jest, let laughter reign,
With fruity jokes that never wane.
In this treat-filled realm so sweet,
Life's a party, what a feat!

Recipes from the Sun

In the garden where laughter grows,
Lemonade giggles, and sunshine glows.
Whisking up smiles with each vibrant splash,
As the ripest fruit does a belly flop crash.

Juggling slices on the picnic table,
Each drippy piece, a funny fable.
Sweet nectar drips from our chins with glee,
Taste-bud tickles from fruity debris.

Who knew a seed could cause such delight?
Making fruit salads feel just so right.
A spoonful of chaos, a dash of flair,
We'll giggle and dance in the sunny air.

Shall we create a zany fruit ball?
Tossing the flavors till one takes a fall.
With the sun as our chef, we take a bite,
Of sheer fruity joy, it feels just right.

The Joyful Strum of Nature

In the orchard where the breezes play,
Fruit strumming tunes in a funny way.
Bananas hum and oranges sing,
Melodies fresh from nature's swing.

Strawberry notes dance on the vine,
With each pluck, they frolic, divine.
The wind whispers jokes between the leaves,
While apple pies boast of sweet reprieves.

A peach sings high, a cherry plays bass,
Tickling our hearts in this fruity space.
A symphony forms in the setting sun,
As nature's jam becomes our fun.

So let's hum along to the fruity spree,
With laughter and joy, we all feel free.
Beneath the trees, our spirits fly,
As tunes of surprise fill the sky.

Confections in the Orchard

Candy bars hiding, oh what a sight,
Layered with laughter under sunlight.
Gummy bears giggle with each little bounce,
While chocolate treats happily renounce.

In this orchard, humor is sweet,
Where candy canes dance on little feet.
Lollipops whisper jokes with a swirl,
Tickling taste buds in a playful twirl.

Peanut butter cups chuckle away,
As we nibble and munch, open to play.
Jellybean quips light up our hearts,
Sharing confection while the fun starts.

So let's gather round with a spoonful of cheer,
Banana splits boisterously near.
With every bite, laughter ensues,
In this fruity world, we never lose.

Mellow Glimmers of Nature’s Bounty

Under the shade, sun drips like honey,
Fruits sitting cozy, all bright and funny.
Watermelons giggle as they roll on by,
In this feast of colors, we reach for the sky.

Cantaloupes chuckle as they bounce off the ground,
With each slice, a melody of laughter is found.
Ripe cantaloupe roars, the sweetness it brings,
Tickling our toes with its joyful flings.

Peaches with blush, giggle with grace,
Twists of delight in this fruity race.
Dancing with sunlight, they sparkle like dreams,
Creating a chorus in bright, creamy streams.

So let’s gather the fruits, both bold and round,
In this blissful orchard, true joy is found.
With chuckles and smiles in harmony,
We munch and we giggle, wild and carefree.

Slices of Sunlight

In the garden, bright and round,
Laughter echoes, joy unbound.
Red and green in summer's glow,
Chasing shadows, to and fro.

Bouncing balls on shiny skin,
Squirrels giggle, let the fun begin.
A slice of joy, a taste so cool,
Become a kid in nature's school.

Juicy drips meet sunny rays,
Sticky fingers, happy days.
Riding waves of fruity cheer,
Bring a friend, spread the cheer.

Peel and cut, such sweet delight,
Everyone's in for a bite!
Sliced in wedges, shared with glee,
Oh, how tasty life can be!

The Richness of Summer's Harvest

Fields abound with nature's treat,
Flavors dance in every beat.
Golden orbs, sun-kissed delight,
Time to munch from day to night.

Chomp and laugh, a fruity spree,
Rolling with joy, just you and me.
Nature's bounty in our hands,
Spinning dreams on golden strands.

Silly seeds, a playful toss,
Who can eat the most? Who's boss?
Sipping juice, oh what a sight,
Sticking tongues out, pure delight!

Gather round, the feast is set,
Funny faces, no regrets.
Summer's treasure, hear the call,
Take a slice, let's share it all!

Fruitsong in the Air

Whistling tunes, a fruity song,
Dancing melodies all day long.
Banana splits sing high and bright,
Watermelon wishes take flight.

Swinging vines sway to the beat,
Juicy notes, oh what a treat!
Frogs in hats, they join the band,
Giggling under fruit-filled land.

Syrupy sweetness fills the air,
Sticky hands are everywhere.
Fruits collide in a playful way,
Chasing laughter till the end of day.

So let's sing, and let's shout,
Join the fruits in a joyful rout.
In this garden, life is fair,
With fruits all around, nothing can compare!

Golden Strings of Sweetness

Cotton candy clouds above,
Summer whispers tales of love.
Strings of gold in every bite,
Crafted joy, pure delight.

Laughter bubbles, sweetness flows,
Funny faces where the breeze blows.
A patchwork quilt of sunny cheer,
Fruits of fun are gathered here.

Dance around the picnic spread,
Funny hats atop each head.
Strum the strings of flavors sweet,
Life's a song, oh what a treat!

So grab a slice, let laughter ring,
Join the chorus, let us sing.
With every bite, our hearts will gleam,
Wrapped in sweetness, life's a dream!

www.ingramcontent.com/pod-product-compliance
Lightning Source LLC
Chambersburg PA
CBHW050306120526
44590CB00016B/2515
* 9 7 8 1 8 0 5 8 6 7 5 3 1 *